Orton Gillingham Decodable 2nd Grade Readers

Easy decodable texts to improve reading and writing skills
in struggling readers and kids with dyslexia

BrainChild

Introduction

Teaching a child with dyslexia to read: Dyslexia is a specific and persistent learning disability that affects reading and writing. For children with dyslexia, learning to read and write can be a difficult challenge for families and educators to tackle. For these children, written language becomes a great barrier, often without meaning or logic, which generates rejection of the task, frustration and discomfort.

The child with dyslexia is a child who has significant difficulties in reading and writing, because their brain processes information differently than other children; which is why if we expect the same results following the traditional method, we will find many barriers that can and often do harm the child. It is important to become aware of the characteristics of this difficulty, so as to help the child learn to read and the consequent overcoming of their difficulties such as understanding, knowledge and attention to their needs.

Reading difficulties with dyslexia

Dyslexia is a learning disability of neurobiological origin, which causes seem to be in the maturation and structuring of certain brain structures.

Dyslexia is therefore a condition of the brain which causes it to process information differently, making it difficult for the person to understand letters, their sounds, their combinations, etc.

Human language is a language based on signs, letters and their sounds, which are arbitrary. The correspondence of each grapheme (letter) with its phoneme (sound), does not follow any logic; it's simply chance. This is one of the greatest difficulties that children face when they have to learn to read and write. Converting the spoken language, they know into signs and transforming sounds into letters is a challenge.

This is even more complicated in children with dyslexia; the relationship becomes something indecipherable for them. No matter how hard they try, they cannot make sense of that dance between letters and sounds. Children with dyslexia have a lot of difficulty recognizing letters; sometimes they mistake letters for others, write them backwards, etc.

Another difficulty they face, is knowing the sound that corresponds to each letter; and things get even more complicated when we combine several letters and we have to know several sounds.

New words are a challenge for them and they can forget them easily, so they must work hard to acquire them. Sometimes they read certain words effortlessly, but the next day they completely forget them.

When they write, they omit letters, change their position, forget words in a sentence, etc.

Dyslexia also affects reading comprehension. When they read they are trying really hard to decipher and understand each word, sometimes even each letter; that is why the meaning of the text gets lost.

Reading comprehension: Activities to help develop it in children

How to teach a child with dyslexia to read

A child with dyslexia has difficulty learning to read and write, because it is hard for them to recognize letters and know which sound they correspond to. However, the child can learn to read and write and overcome those difficulties.

Remember that dyslexia is a learning difficulty that does not imply any physical or mental handicap; the child with dyslexia has adequate capacities. In order to teach a child with dyslexia to read, it is essential to know the nature of their difficulties, understand them and use a teaching method that responds to their needs.

A child with dyslexia

A teaching method to help a child with dyslexia read.

In the first place, it is necessary to make an assessment of the child, to know their reading and writing level, the nature and characteristics of their difficulties in order to understand their specific needs. For this, it is advisable to seek a specialist.

Reading favors the development of phonological awareness (which consists of the correspondence of the sound with the letter). To do this, start with simple activities, letter by letter. Even if other children around the same age read full texts, it may be necessary to start working letter by letter. Later, we can continue with the words, phrases and texts. It is about dedicating more time and more detail to the learning process.

Phonological awareness worksheets

Use motivational activities that are engaging. Do not limit the child to just paper and pencil: they can make letters out of play dough, write on sand with their fingers, play catch or games such as hangman, word searches, crossword puzzles, etc.
Don't force them to read or read a lot. Try to have them read on a daily basis, little by little; sometimes a sentence or a paragraph is enough. Help them understand what they read, ask them questions, ask them to read again, etc.

TABLE OF CONTENTS

Jack and Zack

Once upon a time, there was a little boy named Jack who lived in a cozy little cottage in the countryside. Every day, Jack would wake up early and play outside with his best friend, a lively little black and white spotted puppy named Zack.

One morning, Jack and Zack decided to go on an adventure through the forest to see what they could find. They packed a lunch of sandwiches, but it lacked something. Zack brought some snacks from the rack in the kitchen, put the snacks in the lunch box and set off into the woods.

As they walked, they saw all sorts of interesting things like a family of ducks swimming in a pond and singing a beautiful song while saying, "Quack, quack!" They also saw a beautiful, black-colored butterfly fluttering through the trees, a few children riding their bicycles on a track, and a giant oak tree with a rope swing hanging from one of its branches.

But the best discovery of all was a secret cave hidden behind a big rock. Inside, they found a backpack filled with shiny gold coins and sparkling jewels.

Jack and Zack were so excited; they couldn't wait to show their friends the treasure. So, they carefully closed the backpack and carried it back to the cottage to share with their friends.

From that day on, Jack and Zack were the happiest and luckiest in the whole wide world, thanks to their special backpack and their adventures in the forest.

Write all the 'ack' words that you have found in the story.				

ack

Jack and Zack

- Once upon a time, there was a little boy named _____ who lived in a cozy little cottage in the countryside.
- Every day, Jack would wake up early and play outside with his best friend, a lively little black and white spotted puppy named _____.
- They _____ed a lunch of sandwiches, but it _____ed something.
- Zack brought some _____s from the r_____ in the kitchen, put the snacks in the lunch box, and set off into the woods.
- As they walked, they saw all sorts of interesting things like a family of ducks swimming in a pond and singing a beautiful song while saying, "_____, _____!"
- They also saw a beautiful, _____-colored butterfly fluttering through the trees.
- A few children riding their bicycles on a _____.
- Inside, they found a _____ filled with shiny gold coins and sparkling jewels.
- Jack and Zack were the happiest and luckiest in the whole wide world, thanks to their special _____ and their adventures in the forest.

Write any ten 'ack' words.				

Read the story and circle whether the statement is true or false. If the statement is false, provide the correct answer for it.

Jack is the name of a dog.

True   False

_____

_____

Zack is the name of a boy.

True   False

_____

_____

Jack lived in the city.

True   False

_____

_____

Zack brought some snacks from the cabinet in the kitchen.

True   False

_____

_____

Jack and Zack found a treasure chest.

True   False

_____

_____

Read the story 'Jack and Zack' and answer the following questions.

ack

Where does Jack live?

_____

_____

_____

_____

Who lives with Jack in the cottage?

_____

_____

_____

_____

_____

What does Jack do every day after waking up?

_____

_____

_____

_____

_____

What interesting things did Jack and Zack see in the forest?

_____

_____

_____

_____

_____

Assess the fluency by writing the number of words read per minute.

'ack'

Once upon a time, there was a little boy named Jack who lived in a cozy little cottage in the countryside.	21
Every day, Jack would wake up early and play outside with his best friend, a lively little black and white spotted puppy named Zack.	45
One morning, Jack and Zack decided to go on an adventure through the forest to see what they could find.	65
They packed a lunch of sandwiches, but it lacked something.	75
Zack brought some snacks from the rack in the kitchen, put the snacks in the lunch box, and set off into the woods.	98
As they walked, they saw all sorts of interesting things like a family of ducks swimming in a pond and singing a beautiful song while saying, "Quack, quack!"	126
They also saw a beautiful, black-colored butterfly fluttering through the trees, a few children riding their bicycles on a track, and a giant oak tree with a rope swing hanging from one of its branches.	161
But the best discovery of all was a secret cave hidden behind a big rock. Inside, they found a backpack filled with shiny gold coins and sparkling jewels.	189
Jack and Zack were so excited; they couldn't wait to show their friends the treasure.	204
So, they carefully closed the backpack and carried it back to the cottage to share with their friends.	222
From that day on, Jack and Zack were the happiest and luckiest in the whole wide world, thanks to their special backpack and their adventures in the forest.	250

Date			
Words per minute			
Number of Errors			

Make sentences using the words written below.

Backpack

_____
_____

Rack

_____
_____

Sack

_____
_____

Lack

_____
_____

Back

_____
_____

Quack

_____
_____

Make a story using any of the following five words.

ack

Jack   Zack   Rack   Back
Pack   Lack   Track
Sack   Crack   Stack

_____

_____

_____

_____

_____

_____

_____

_____

Write the correct word matching
its picture.

ck

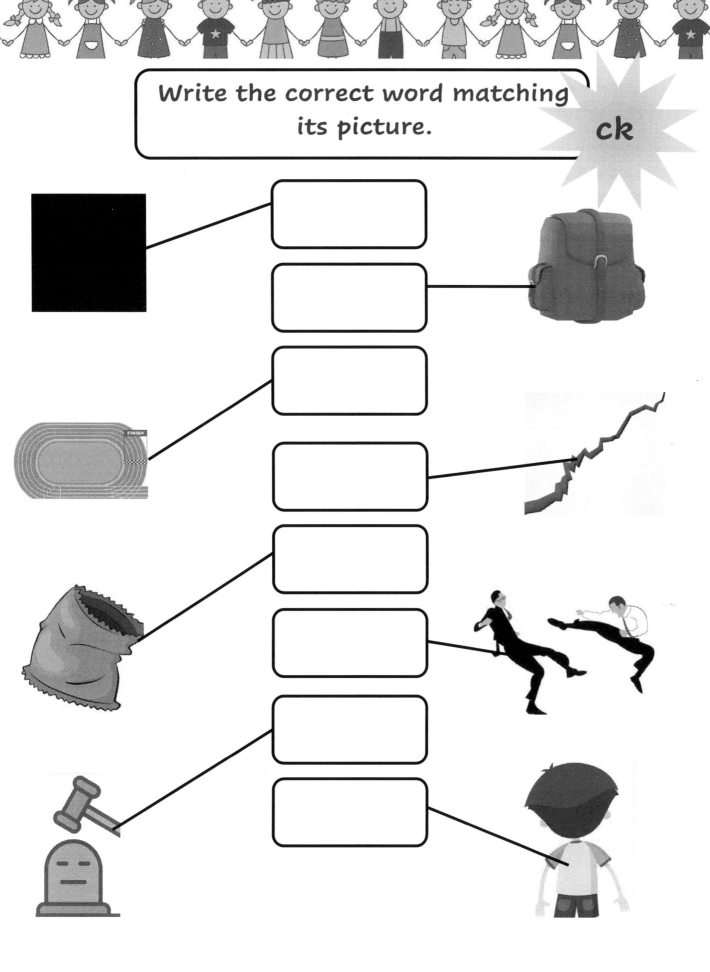

8

Write the name of each picture and listen to the ending sound. Circle 'ack' or 'ock'.

ack

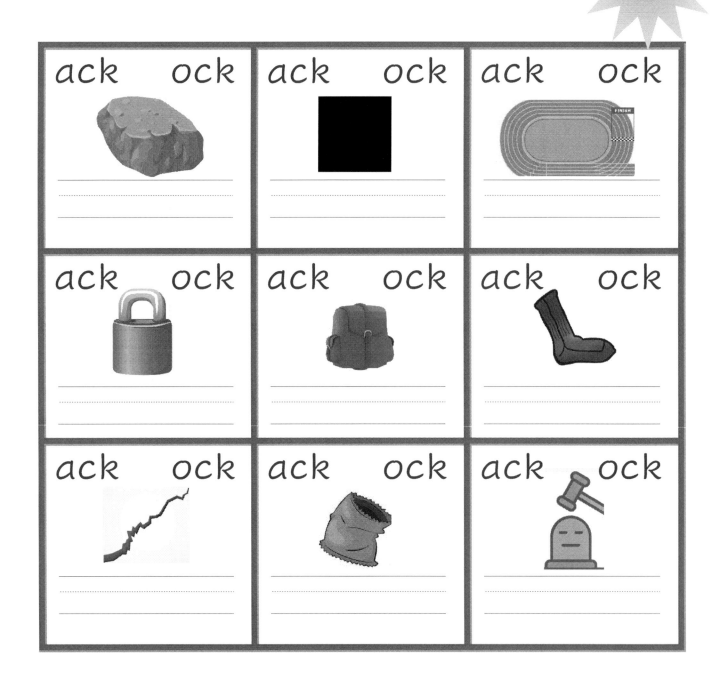

ack ock	ack ock	ack ock
ack ock	ack ock	ack ock
ack ock	ack ock	ack ock

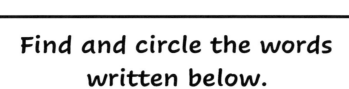

Find and circle the words written below.

ack

track   pack   lack   sack
whack   smack   backpack
track   hack   back

t	h	k	n	o	c	k	p
h	r	d	e	c	k	k	l
a	g	a	w	h	i	p	a
t	r	a	c	K	v	m	c
w	h	a	c	k	n	s	k
c	p	a	c	k	v	i	e
k	f	j	d	o	c	k	l
e	r	o	c	k	m	w	k

Read the story. Identify and underline all the 'ant' words.

'ant'

Visit to the city

There was once a little girl named Grace who lived in a small village in the countryside. Grace loved to play outside and explore the woods and fields around her house. She was especially fond of plants and often spent hours tending to her garden and trying to grow the biggest and best flowers.

One day, Grace's mom asked her, "What do you want for your birthday?" Grace said, "I want to visit my grandma." Mom told Grace that they were going on a special trip to the city to visit her grandma. Grace was so excited that she couldn't wait to pack her suitcase; she put on her favorite blue pants and a pink shirt that her grandma gave her and got on the road.

When they arrived at grandma's house, Grace was amazed by all the tall buildings and busy streets. She had never been to the city before and there was so much to see and do.

Grandma took Grace and her mom on a special tour of the city, showing them all the fun places to visit like the botanical garden, the park, and the museum. They even went to a big concert in the park where they danced and sang along to the music.

As they walked through the city, Grace couldn't help but notice all the beautiful plants and flowers that were growing everywhere. She saw elegant rose bushes, giant sunflowers, and tiny ants crawling through the grass.

Grace was so inspired by all the plants that she couldn't wait to get back home and start growing her own garden. She knew that with a little bit of hard work and patience, she could grow the most beautiful flowers in the whole wide world.

Write all the 'ant' words that you have found in the story.				

Visit to the city

ant

- There was once a little girl named _____ who lived in a small village in the countryside.
- She was especially fond of _____ and often spent hours tending to her garden and trying to grow the biggest and best flowers.
- One day, Grace's mom asked her, "What do you _____ for your birthday?" Grace said, "I _____ to visit my grandma.".
- Grace was so excited that she couldn't wait to pack her suitcase; she put on her favorite blue _____ and a pink shirt that her grandma gave her and got on the road.
- When they arrived at grandma's house, Grace was amazed by all the _____ buildings and busy streets. She had never been to the _____ before and there was so much to see and do.
- Grace couldn't help but notice all the beautiful _____ and flowers that were growing everywhere. She saw _____ rose bushes, _____ sunflowers, and tiny _____ crawling through the grass.
- Grace was so inspired by all the _____ that she couldn't wait to get back home and start growing her own garden.

Write any ten 'ant' words.				

Read the story and circle whether the statement is true or false. If the statement is false, provide the correct answer for it.

ant

A little girl named Alice lived in a village.

True   False

_____

Grace loved to stay in the house and read books.

True   False

_____

Grace wanted to visit her grandma.

True   False

_____

She put on her favorite red pants.

True   False

_____

She saw beautiful rose bushes, big sunflowers, and tiny insects crawling through the grass.

True   False

_____

Read the story 'Visit to the city' and answer the following questions.

What was the name of the girl in the story and where did she live?

_____

_____

_____

_____

What did Grace like to do all day?

_____

_____

_____

_____

What did Grace want for her birthday?

_____

_____

_____

_____

What did Grace see in the city?

_____

_____

Assess the fluency by writing the number of words read per minute.

'ant'

There was once a little girl named Grace who lived in a small village in the countryside.	17
Grace loved to play outside and explore the woods and fields around her house.	31
She was especially fond of plants and often spent hours tending to her garden and trying to grow the biggest and best flowers.	54
One day, Grace's mom asked her, "What do you want for your birthday?"	67
Grace said, "I want to visit my grandma."	75
Mom told Grace that they were going on a special trip to the city to visit her grandma.	93
Grace was so excited that she couldn't wait to pack her suitcase; she put on her favorite blue pants and a pink shirt that her grandma gave her and got on the road.	126
When they arrived at grandma's house, Grace was amazed by all the tall buildings and busy streets.	143
She had never been to the city before and there was so much to see and do.	160
Grandma took Grace and her mom on a special tour of the city, showing them all the fun places to visit like the botanical garden, the park, and the museum.	190
They even went to a big concert in the park where they danced and sang along to the music.	209
As they walked through the city, Grace couldn't help but notice all the beautiful plants and flowers that were growing everywhere.	230
She saw elegant rose bushes, giant sunflowers, and tiny ants crawling through the grass.	244
Grace was so inspired by all the plants that she couldn't wait to get back home and start growing her own garden	266
She knew that with a little bit of hard work and patience, she could grow the most beautiful flowers in the whole wide world.	290

Date			
Words per minute			
Number of Errors			

Ant

_____

- -

_____

Rant

_____

- -

_____

Pant

_____

- -

_____

Want

_____

- -

_____

Important

_____

- -

_____

Plant

_____

- -

_____

Make a story using any of the following five words.

'ant'

Ant	Plant	Want	Pant
Rant	Slant	Grant	Chant
	Giant	Distant	

_____
- -
_____

_____
- -
_____

_____
- -
_____

_____
- -
_____

_____
- -
_____

_____
- -
_____

Write the correct word matching its picture.

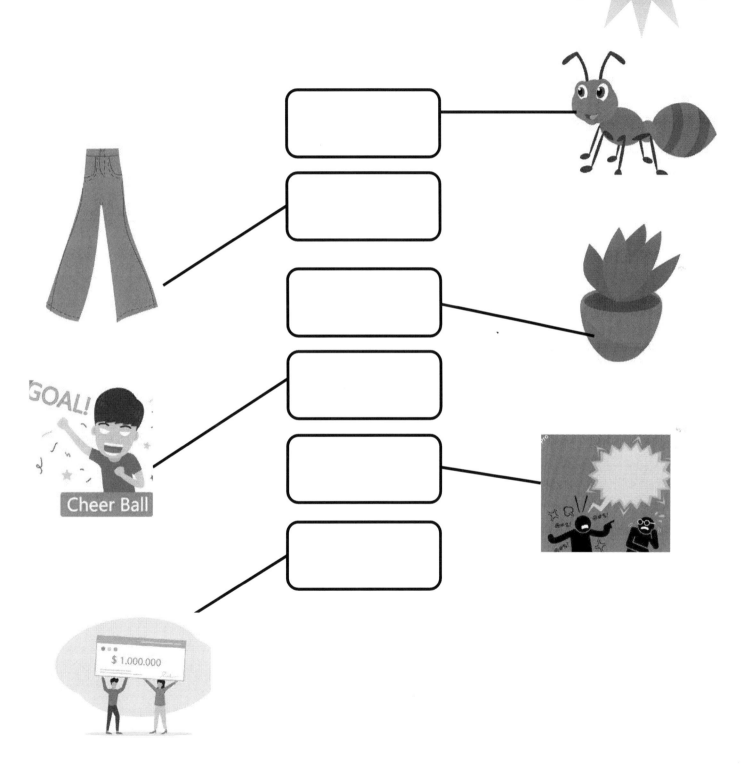

Cheer Ball

GOAL!

$ 1.000.000

Write the name of each picture and listen to the ending sound. Circle 'ack' or 'ant'.

'ant'

ack ant	ack ant	ack ant
ack ant	ack ant	ack ant
ack ant	ack ant	ack ant

Find and circle the words written below.

'ant'

Pant	Grant	Cant
distant	Rant	Want	Slant

d	g	r	a	n	t	k	p
i	r	c	e	c	k	k	l
s	g	a	w	h	i	p	a
t	r	n	c	K	v	m	t
a	h	t	c	k	n	t	n
n	p	a	n	t	v	n	a
t	f	j	d	o	c	a	l
e	r	a	n	t	m	w	s

Read the story. Identify and underline all the 'ad' words. 'ad'

Brad's adventure

Once upon a time, in a small village by the sea, there lived a young boy named Brad. Brad loved to explore and have adventures, but he always made sure to stay safe.

One day, Brad was a bit sad and decided to go on a hike through the forest to a hidden waterfall that he had heard about from his dad. He said to himself, "It is a bad idea to go un-prepared." So, he packed a bag with a map, a flashlight, and some snacks and set off early in the morning.

He felt glad as he hiked through the woods. Brad saw all sorts of amazing sights like a lad of deer grazing in a meadow, a bright red cardinal singing in a tree, and a family of rabbits hopping through the underbrush.

But the best part of the hike was when Brad finally reached the hidden waterfall. It was a beautiful sight, with the water cascading down a rocky cliff into a crystal-clear pool below.

Brad sat by the pool and ate his snacks, enjoying the peaceful sound of the falling water. When it was time to go home, Brad carefully marked his map and retraced his steps back to the village.

He couldn't wait to tell all his friends about his amazing adventure and the beautiful waterfall he had discovered.

Write all the 'ad' words that you have found in the story.				

Read the story and fill in the blank spaces with the appropriate words.

'ad'

Brad's adventure

- Once upon a time, in a small village by the sea, there lived a young boy named _____.
- One day, Brad was a bit _____ and decided to go on a hike through the forest to a hidden waterfall that he had heard about from his _____.
- He said to himself, "It is a _____ idea to go un-prepared."
- So, he packed a _____ with a _____, a flashlight, and some snacks and set off early in the morning.
- He felt _____ as he hiked through the woods.
- Brad saw all sorts of amazing sights like a _____ of _____ grazing in a meadow, a bright red cardinal singing in a tree, and a family of rabbits hopping through the underbrush.
- But the best part of the hike was when Brad finally reached the hidden _____.
- It was a beautiful sight, with the water cascading down a rocky _____ into a crystal-clear pool below.
- Brad carefully marked his _____ and retraced his steps back to the village.

Write any ten 'ad' words.				

22

Read the story and circle whether the statement is true or false. If the statement is false, provide the correct answer for it.

'ad'

Brad lives in the city.

True   False

_____

Brad heard a story about a hidden waterfall from his mom.

True   False

_____

Brad loved to explore and have adventures.

True   False

_____

Brad saw all sorts of amazing sights like a family of deer grazing on a hill.

True   False

_____

_____

Brad carefully marked his map.

True   False

_____

Read the story 'Brad's adventures' and answer the following questions.

What is the name of the boy in the story? Where does he live?

_____

_____

_____

What does Brad like to do?

_____

_____

_____

What did Brad hear from his dad?

_____

_____

_____

What interesting things did Brad see on the way to the waterfall?

_____

_____

_____

Assess the fluency by writing the number of words read per minute.

'ad'

Once upon a time, in a small village by the sea, there lived a young boy named Brad.	18
Brad loved to explore and have adventures, but he always made sure to stay safe.	33
One day, Brad was a bit sad and decided to go on a hike through the forest to a hidden waterfall that he had heard about from his dad.	62
He said to himself, "It is a bad idea to go un-prepared."	74
So, he packed a bag with a map, a flashlight, and some snacks and set off early in the morning.	94
He felt glad as he hiked through the woods. Brad saw all sorts of amazing sights like a lad of deer grazing in a meadow, a bright red cardinal singing in a tree, and a family of rabbits hopping through the underbrush.	136
But the best part of the hike was when Brad finally reached the hidden waterfall.	151
It was a beautiful sight, with the water cascading down a rocky cliff into a crystal-clear pool below.	169
Brad sat by the pool and ate his snacks, enjoying the peaceful sound of the falling water.	186
When it was time to go home, Brad carefully marked his map and retraced his steps back to the village.	206
He couldn't wait to tell all his friends about his amazing adventure and the beautiful waterfall he had discovered.	225

Date			
Words per minute			
Number of Errors			

Make sentences using the words written below.

'ad'

Bad

_____

Had

_____

Sad

_____

Lad

_____

Mad

_____

Brad

_____

Bad   Mad   Had   Sad   Lad

Glad   Dad   Pad

_____
- -
_____

_____
- -
_____

_____
- -
_____

_____
- -
_____

_____
- -
_____

_____
- -
_____

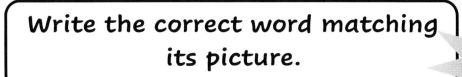

Write the correct word matching its picture.

'ad'

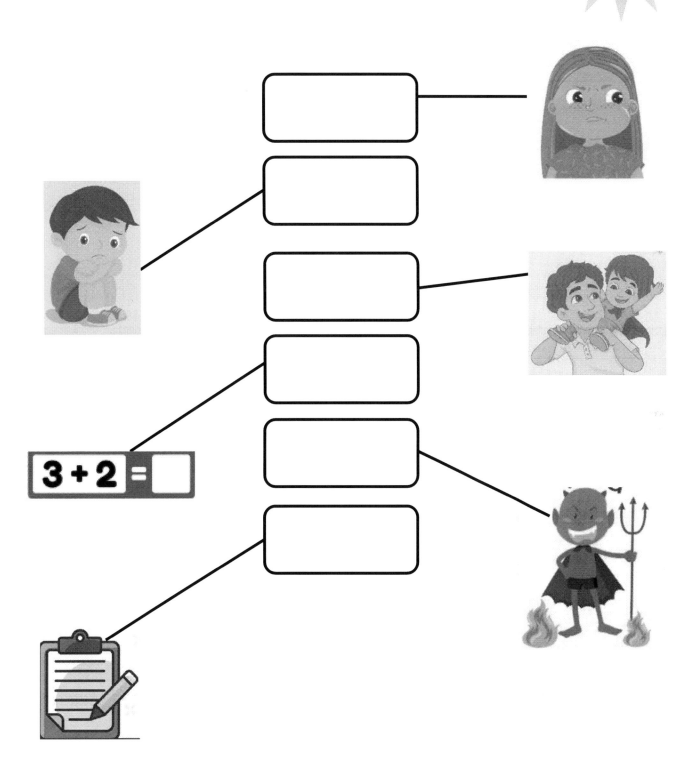

Write the name of each picture and listen to the ending sound. Circle 'ant' or 'ad'.

'ad'

ant ad	ant ad	ant ad
_____	_____	_____
ant ad	ant ad	ant ad
_____	_____	_____
ant ad	ant ad	ant ad
_____	_____	_____

Find and circle the words written below.

'ad'

bad   pad   had   sad
lad   glad   dad

b	h	d	n	o	c	k	p
h	a	d	e	c	k	k	l
p	g	d	w	h	a	d	a
t	r	a	c	K	v	a	c
w	h	a	c	d	n	s	k
c	p	a	a	k	v	i	d
k	g	l	a	d	c	a	l
e	r	o	c	k	d	w	k

The special bag

The little boy had a special bag; it was vibrant red with a tag attached to it. The bag was a present from his grandmother. Whenever he felt down, the bag cheered him up.

Every day when school ended, the young boy would take out his rag and drag it around town. He'd clean every windowsill and stoop, earning money for the family.

When it was time to go home and tell his parents about the work he had done, the little boy would gag in shock when he found out how much he earned. But with a wag of his rag, he was happy to help his family.

He continued this routine every day, and even though it was tiresome, he felt a sense of pride whenever his parents thanked him.

One day, the little boy decided to take out some of the money from his bag. He gave half of it to his family and spent the other half on himself. He went to the park and bought candy, toys, and books.

The little boy now had a special bag filled with memories, full of all the hard work he had done for his family. From that day on, he was never afraid to show his bag around town. It reminded him of how much his loved ones meant to him and that no matter what happened, he would always have a home in the red bag.

Write all the 'ag' words that you have found in the story.				

Read the story and fill in the blank spaces with the appropriate words.

'ag'

The special bag

- The little boy had a special _____.
- it was vibrant red with a _____ attached to it. The ____ was a present from his grandmother.
- Every day when school ended, the young boy would take out his _____ and _____ it around town.
- He'd clean every windowsill and stoop, earning _____ for the family.
- When it was time to go home and tell his parents about the work he had done, the little boy would _____ in shock when he found out how much he earned.
- But with a _____ of his _____, he was happy to help his family.
- One day, the little boy decided to take out some of the money from his _____.
- He gave half of it to his family and spent the other _____ on himself.
- The little boy now had a special _____ filled with memories, full of all the hard work he had done for his family.

Write any ten 'ag' words.				

32

Read the story and circle whether the statement is true or false. If the statement is false, provide the correct answer for it.

'ag'

The little boy had a special sack.

True   False

_____

_____

It was vibrant blue with a tag.

True   False

_____

_____

The bag was a gift from his dad.

True   False

_____

_____

Every day when school ended, the young boy would take out his cloth and drag it around town.

True   False

_____

_____

_____

But with a wag of his rag he was happy to help his family.

True   False

_____

Read the story 'The special bag' and answer the following questions.

'ag'

What did the boy have?

_____

_____

_____

What did the bag look like and who gave the bag to the little boy?

_____

_____

_____

What did the boy use to do?

_____

_____

_____

What did the boy do with the money he earned?

_____

_____

_____

Assess the fluency by writing the number of words read per minute.

'ag'

The little boy had a special bag; it was vibrant red with a tag attached to it.	17
The bag was a present from his grandmother.	25
Whenever he felt down, the bag cheered him up.	34
Every day when school ended, the young boy would take out his rag and drag it around town.	52
He'd clean every windowsill and stoop, earning money for the family.	63
When it was time to go home and tell his parents about the work he had done, the little boy would gag in shock when he found out how much he earned.	95
But with a wag of his rag, he was happy to help his family.	109
He continued this routine every day, and even though it was tiresome, he felt a sense of pride whenever his parents thanked him.	132
One day, the little boy decided to take out some of the money from his bag.	148
He gave half of it to his family and spent the other half on himself.	163
He went to the park and bought candy, toys, and books.	174
The little boy now had a special bag filled with memories, full of all the hard work he had done for his family.	197
From that day on, he was never afraid to show his bag around town.	211
It reminded him of how much his loved ones meant to him and that no matter what happened, he would always have a home in the red bag.	239

Date			
Words per minute			
Number of Errors			

Bag

_____

_____

Tag

_____

_____

Wag

_____

_____

Gag

_____

_____

Drag

_____

_____

Brag

_____

_____

Make a story using any of the following three words.

'ag'

Gag   Drag   Bag   Wag

Brag   Flag   Swag

_____
- -
_____
- -
_____
- -
_____
- -
_____
- -
_____
- -
_____

Write the correct word matching its picture.

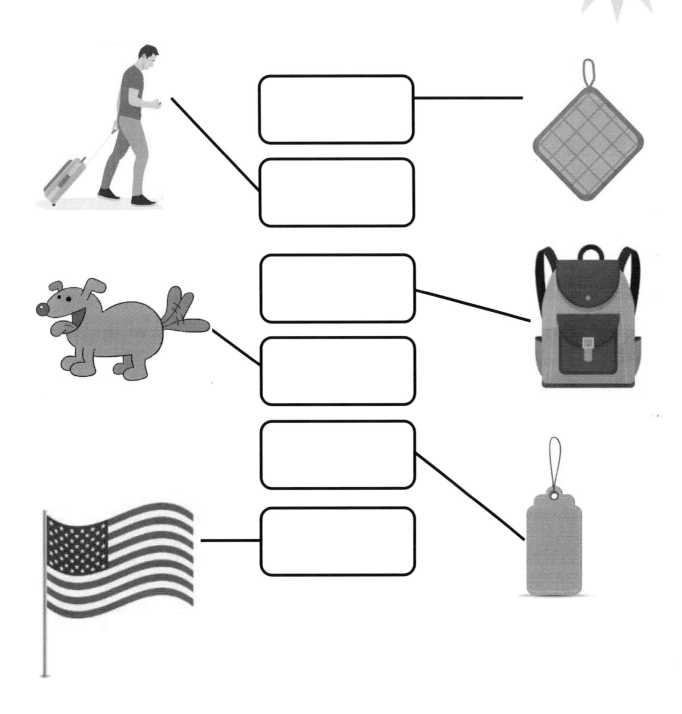

Write the name of each picture and listen to the ending sound. Circle 'ag' or 'ad'.

'ag'

ad	ag	ad	ag	ad	ag
ad	ag	ad	ag	ad	ag
ad	ag	ad	ag	ad	ag

Find and circle the words written below.

'ag'

drag   wag   tag   bag   swag
lag   jag   nag   snag   brag

d	r	a	g	t	c	k	p
h	a	a	e	c	a	k	l
p	w	d	w	b	a	g	a
g	r	a	c	K	v	a	c
a	h	n	c	d	n	s	g
r	p	a	a	k	v	i	a
b	s	n	a	g	c	a	l
e	s	w	a	g	d	w	k

Read the story. Identify and underline all the 'all' words.

'all'

A visit to the mall

It was a typical Saturday morning, and the mall was bustling with people. Rob had been looking forward to this weekend for weeks, so he made his way to the mall early. He strolled slowly through the halls, enjoying watching all the people going in and out of the stores.

Rob stopped at a small stall that was selling unique items. He spent some time looking at all the trinkets but didn't find anything that caught his eye. As he walked away, he felt a sudden urge to turn around and go back, it was as if something in the stall had called out to him.

Confused, Rob went back to the stall and looked around. There, on the wall, he noticed a small glass ball with swirls of purple and green inside it. Somehow, it felt oddly familiar to him. He picked it up and held it in his hands. As he did, memories began flooding back to his mind. He remembered visiting this same mall when he was younger and being mesmerized by the ball. He remembered being so excited to buy it, but his mother had called him away before he could do so. He hadn't thought about that moment for years, yet here it was back in front of him again.

Rob smiled as he recalled how happy the little glass ball had made him feel all those years ago. He decided it was time to take the ball home and make it part of his life. And so, with a renewed sense of joy, Rob paid for the ball and made his way back out into the mall, happy that he had been able to recall this special moment from his past.

Write all the 'all' words that you have found in the story.				

'all'

A visit to the mall

- It was a typical Saturday morning, and the _____ was bustling with people.
- He strolled slowly through the _____, enjoying watching all the people going in and out of the stores.
- Rob stopped at a _____ stall that was selling unique items.
- As he walked away, he felt a sudden urge to turn around and go back, it was as if something in the stall had called out to him.
- Confused, Rob went back to the _____ and looked around.
- There, on the _____, he noticed a small glass ball with swirls of purple and green inside it.
- He decided it was time to take the _____ home and make it part of his life.
- And so, with a renewed sense of joy, Rob paid for the ball and made his way back out into the _____, happy that he had been able to _____ this special moment from his past.

Write any ten 'all' words.				

Read the story and circle whether the statement is true or false. If the statement is false, provide the correct answer for it.

'all'

It was a typical Sunday morning.

True   False

_____

Rob went to the mall.

True   False

_____

Jason saw a small stall.

True   False

_____

There, on the wall, he noticed a small glass ball with swirls of orange and blue inside it.

True   False

_____

He remembered being so excited to buy the ball.

True   False

_____

Read the story 'A visit to the mall' and answer the following questions.

What is the name of the boy in the story and where did he go?

_____

_____

_____

_____

What day was it and was the mall crowded?

_____

_____

_____

_____

What was the small stall selling?

_____

_____

_____

_____

Why did Rob go back to the stall and what caught his attention?

_____

_____

_____

_____

Assess the fluency by writing the number of words read per minute.

'all'

It was a typical Saturday morning, and the mall was bustling with people.	13
Rob had been looking forward to this weekend for weeks, so he made his way to the mall early.	32
He strolled slowly through the halls, enjoying watching all the people going in and out of the stores.	50
Rob stopped at a small stall that was selling unique items.	61
He spent some time looking at all the trinkets but didn't find anything that caught his eye.	78
As he walked away, he felt a sudden urge to turn around and go back, it was as if something in the stall had called out to him.	106
Confused, Rob went back to the stall and looked around.	116
There, on the wall, he noticed a small glass ball with swirls of purple and green inside it.	134
Somehow, it felt oddly familiar to him.	141
He picked it up and held it in his hands. As he did, memories began flooding back to his mind.	161
He remembered visiting this same mall when he was younger and being mesmerized by the ball.	177
He remembered being so excited to buy it, but his mother had called him away before he could do so.	197
He hadn't thought about that moment for years, yet here it was back in front of him again.	215
Rob smiled as he recalled how happy the little glass ball had made him feel all those years ago.	234
He decided it was time to take the ball home and make it part of his life.	251
And so, with a renewed sense of joy, Rob paid for the ball and made his way back out into the mall, happy that he had been able to recall this special moment from his past.	287

Date			
Words per minute			
Number of Errors			

Call

_____
- -
_____

Ball

_____
- -
_____

Recall

_____
- -
_____

Hall

_____
- -
_____

Wall

_____
- -
_____

Mall

_____
- -
_____

Call   Ball   Recall   Hall

Mall   Wall   Small   Stall

All   Tall   Fall   Appall

_____
_____

_____
_____

_____
_____

_____
_____

_____
_____

_____
_____

_____
_____

_____
_____

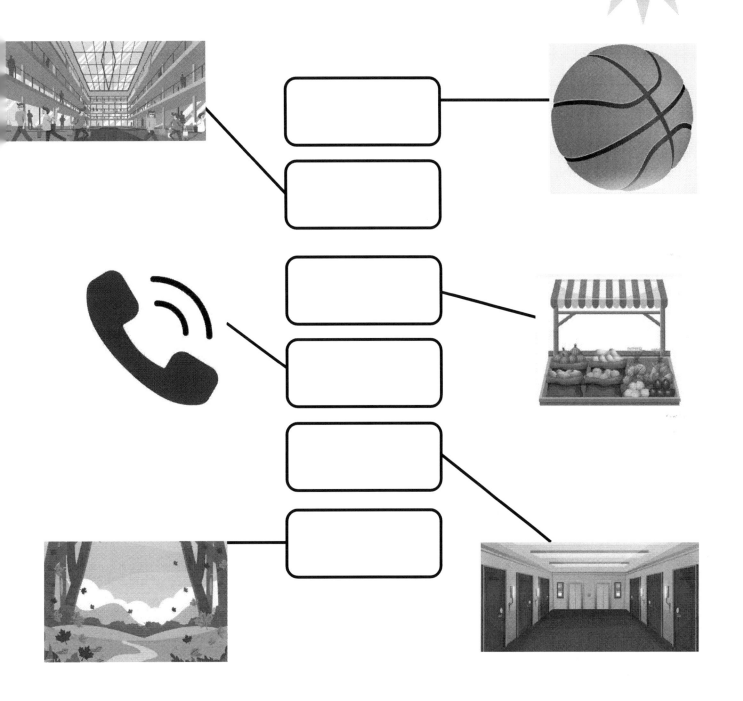

Write the name of each picture and listen to the ending sound. Circle 'ag' or 'all'.

'all'

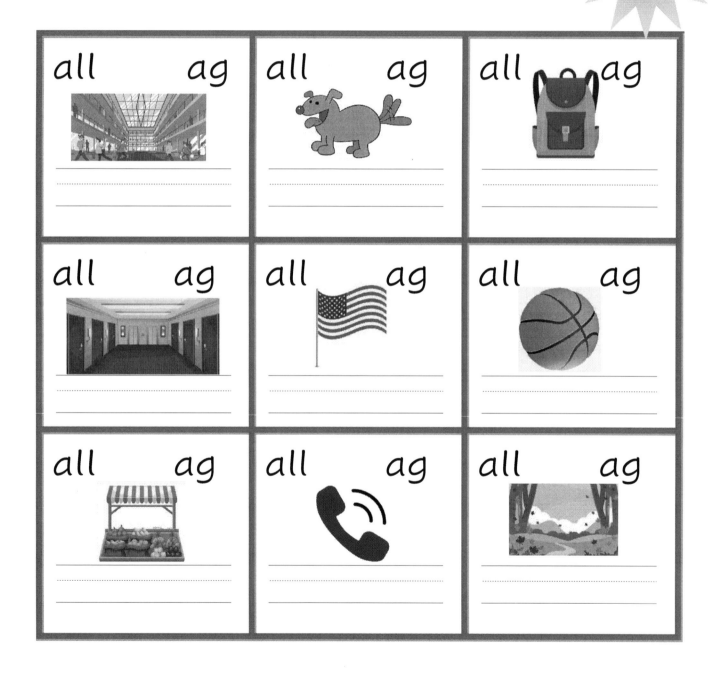

all	ag	all	ag	all	ag
all	ag	all	ag	all	ag
all	ag	all	ag	all	ag

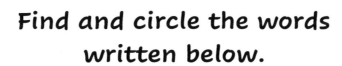

Find and circle the words written below.

'all'

Stall   mall   call   ball   fall
small   appall   tall   hall

h	r	a	l	t	c	k	a
h	a	l	e	c	a	k	p
p	a	l	w	b	a	g	p
t	c	a	l	l	v	a	a
l	b	a	l	l	n	s	l
l	p	a	a	k	l	i	l
a	s	t	a	l	l	a	l
m	s	m	a	l	l	w	f

Read the story. Identify and underline all the 'amp' words. **'amp'**

Champ's mysterious adventure

Once upon a time, there lived a poor boy named Champ. He lived in the outskirts of town, near an abandoned camp. Every day he would go to the camp to explore and play with his friends. One day while exploring, he stumbled upon a ramp that led deep into the forest. Intrigued by this mysterious structure, he walked up the ramp and wandered into the woods.

He soon found himself in a strange clearing, with a lamp hanging from one of the trees. He walked closer to inspect it but was startled when he heard a loud stamp coming from behind him. Turning around, he saw an old tramp standing there, looking at him with suspicion.

The tramp spoke in a gruff voice, telling Champ he was trespassing and needed to leave. Terrified, Champ ran back down the ramp and out of the woods as fast as he could. He felt a cramp in his side from running so hard and soon realized how damp his clothes were from all the sweat.

Once he was home, Champ told his family about the strange tramp and ramp he had found. From then on, every time they heard a loud stamp or saw a lamp in the woods, they remembered Champ's mysterious adventure, and all ran away together.

Write all the 'amp' words that you have found in the story.				

Read the story and fill in the blank spaces with the appropriate words.

'amp'

Champ's mysterious adventure

- Once upon a time, there lived a poor boy named _____.
- He lived in the outskirts of town, near an abandoned _____.
- Every day he would go to the _____ to explore and play with his friends.
- One day while exploring, he stumbled upon a _____ that led deep into the forest.
- Intrigued by this mysterious structure, he walked up the _____ and wandered into the woods.
- He soon found himself in a strange clearing, with a _____ hanging from one of the trees.
- He walked closer to inspect it but was startled when he heard a loud _____ coming from behind him.
- Turning around, he saw an old _____ standing there, looking at him with suspicion.
- The _____ spoke in a gruff voice, telling Champ he was trespassing and needed to leave.

Write any ten 'amp' words.				

52

Read the story and circle whether the statement is true or false. If the statement is false, provide the correct answer for it.

Champ was a rich boy.

True   False

_____

_____

Champ lived in the countryside.

True   False

_____

_____

Champ lived near an abandoned camp.

True   False

_____

_____

One day while exploring, he stumbled upon a rock that led deep into the forest.

True   False

_____

_____

_____

He soon found himself in a strange clearing, with a lamp hanging from one of the trees.

True   False

_____

_____

Read the story 'Champ's mysterious adventure' and answer the following questions.

'amp'

What is the name of the boy in the story and where did he live?

_____
_____
_____
_____

What did Champ like to do?

_____
_____
_____
_____

What happened one day during his adventure? Explain in detail.

_____
_____
_____
_____
_____
_____
_____

Assess the fluency by writing the number of words read per minute.

'amp'

Once upon a time, there lived a poor boy named Champ.	11
He lived in the outskirts of town, near an abandoned camp.	22
Every day he would go to the camp to explore and play with his friends.	37
One day while exploring, he stumbled upon a ramp that led deep into the forest.	52
Intrigued by this mysterious structure, he walked up the ramp and wandered into the woods.	67
He soon found himself in a strange clearing, with a lamp hanging from one of the trees.	84
He walked closer to inspect it but was startled when he heard a loud stamp coming from behind him.	103
Turning around, he saw an old tramp standing there, looking at him with suspicion.	117
The tramp spoke in a gruff voice, telling Champ he was trespassing and needed to leave.	133
Terrified, Champ ran back down the ramp and out of the woods as fast as he could.	150
He felt a cramp in his side from running so hard and soon realized how damp his clothes were from all the sweat.	173
Once he was home, Champ told his family about the strange tramp and ramp he had found.	190
From then on, every time they heard a loud stamp or saw a lamp in the woods, they remembered Champ's mysterious adventure, and all ran away together.	217

Date			
Words per minute			
Number of Errors			

Champ

_____

_____

Cramp

_____

_____

Tramp

_____

_____

Lamp

_____

_____

Ramp

_____

_____

Damp

_____

_____

Make a story using any of the following three words. 'amp'

Champ Tramp Cramp

Damp Lamp Ramp

Clamp Stamp Camp

Write the correct word matching its picture.

'amp'

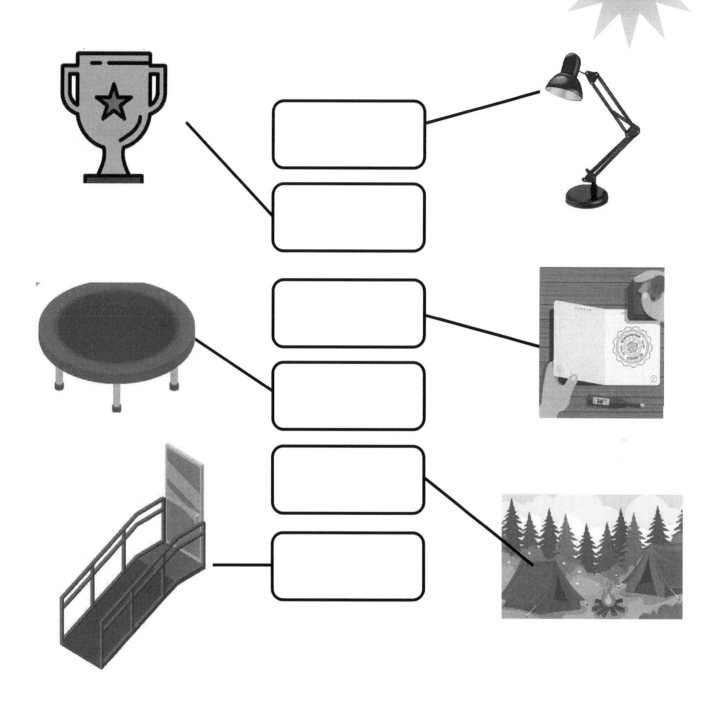

Write the name of each picture and listen to the ending sound. Circle 'amp' or 'all'.

'amp'

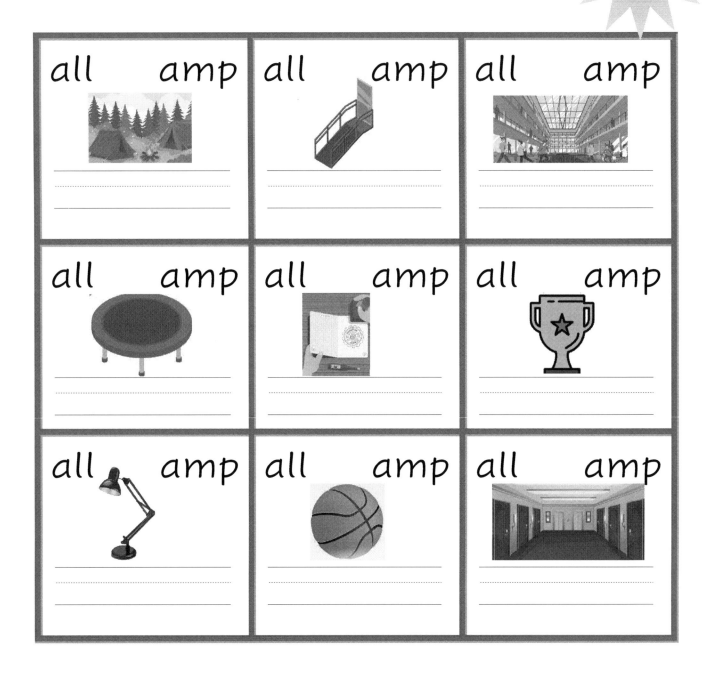

all amp	all amp	all amp
all amp	all amp	all amp
all amp	all amp	all amp

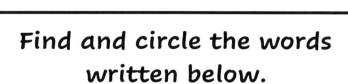

Find and circle the words written below.

'amp'

Stamp   camp   lamp   ramp
Tramp   champ   clamp

h	r	c	l	t	c	k	a
s	t	a	m	p	a	k	p
p	a	m	w	b	a	g	p
t	c	p	l	l	v	a	m
l	a	m	p	l	n	s	a
c	l	a	m	p	l	i	h
a	s	t	r	a	m	p	c
m	s	m	p	m	a	r	t

Pam and Sam

Sam was a lonely boy. He had always felt out of place in the world, no matter where he went. His best friend Pam tried to lift his spirits, but nothing seemed to work. One day, they were walking along the beach and noticed an old, abandoned dam with a strange glow emanating from within.

Curious, Pam and Sam decided to investigate. As they explored the old dam, they stumbled upon an ancient yam tree with fruits of all colors. Pam plucked a yellow one from the branch and took a bite. She immediately began to glow with a beautiful golden aura. Sam was amazed at what he saw and plucked a purple one for himself. When he bit into it, he too was illuminated with a deep violet hue.

The two friends laughed and embraced each other in joy. Suddenly, they heard a loud slam behind them. Turning around, they saw an old man demanding to know why Sam and Pam had taken from the tree without his permission. He instructed them to put all the yams back, and then tried to punish them by making them eat a plate of slimy ham.

Sam and Pam were filled with fear, but they refused to give in. So instead of eating the slimy ham, Sam asked if he could offer his own dish as payment for taking the yams. The old man agreed, and so Sam cooked up a delicious batch of jam. The old man was so impressed by Sam's cooking that he forgave them and allowed the two to keep all the yams they had collected.

From then on, Sam and Pam ventured back to the dam every week to pick more yams. And while they did, they shared stories and laughed, feeling more connected than ever before. With the help of the yams, Sam and Pam had found a way to connect with each other, and with the world around them.

Write all the 'am' words that you have found in the story.				

Pam and Sam

- _____ was a lonely boy.
- His best friend _____ tried to lift his spirits.
- One day, they were walking along the beach and noticed an old, abandoned _____ with a strange glow emanating from within.
- As they explored the old dam, they stumbled upon an ancient _____ tree with fruits of all colors.
- _____ plucked a yellow one from the branch and took a bite.
- _____ was amazed at what he saw and plucked a purple one for himself.
- They heard a loud _____ behind them.
- Turning around, they saw an old man demanding to know why _____ and _____ had taken from the tree without his permission.
- So instead of eating the slimy _____, Sam asked if he could offer his own dish as payment for taking the yams.
- The old man agreed, and so Sam cooked up a delicious batch of _____.

Write any ten 'am' words.				

Read the story and circle whether the statement is true or false. If the statement is false, provide the correct answer for it.

James was a lonely boy.

True   False

_____

Sam's best friend was Oliver.

True   False

_____

One day they saw an old, abandoned dam.

True   False

_____

They stumbled upon an ancient palm tree with fruits of all colors.

True   False

_____

Sam cooked up a delicious batch of clam.

True   False

_____

What are the names of the characters in the story?

_____

_____

_____

_____

What did Sam and Pam notice on the beach?

_____

_____

_____

_____

What did Sam and Pam explore on the dam? Explain in detail.

_____

_____

_____

_____

_____

_____

_____

Sam was a lonely boy.	5
He had always felt out of place in the world, no matter where he went.	20
His best friend Pam tried to lift his spirits, but nothing seemed to work.	34
One day, they were walking along the beach and noticed an old, abandoned dam with a strange glow emanating from within.	55
Curious, Pam and Sam decided to investigate.	62
As they explored the old dam, they stumbled upon an ancient yam tree with fruits of all colors.	80
Pam plucked a yellow one from the branch and took a bite.	92
She immediately began to glow with a beautiful golden aura.	102
Sam was amazed at what he saw and plucked a purple one for himself.	116
When he bit into it, he too was illuminated with a deep violet hue.	130
The two friends laughed and embraced each other in joy.	140
Suddenly, they heard a loud slam behind them.	148
Turning around, they saw an old man demanding to know why Sam and Pam had taken from the tree without his permission.	170
He instructed them to put all the yams back, and then tried to punish them by making them eat a plate of slimy ham.	194
Sam and Pam were filled with fear, but they refused to give in.	207
So instead of eating the slimy ham, Sam asked if he could offer his own dish as payment for taking the yams.	229
The old man agreed, and so Sam cooked up a delicious batch of jam.	243
The old man was so impressed by Sam's cooking that he forgave them and allowed the two to keep all the yams they had collected.	268
From then on, Sam and Pam ventured back to the dam every week to pick more yams.	285
And while they did, they shared stories and laughed, feeling more connected than ever before.	300
With the help of the yams, Sam and Pam had found a way to connect with each other, and with the world around them.	324

Date			
Words per minute			
Number of Errors			

Jam

_____

- - - - - - - - - - - - - - - - - -

_____

Yam

_____

- - - - - - - - - - - - - - - - - -

_____

Cram

_____

- - - - - - - - - - - - - - - - - -

_____

Tram

_____

- - - - - - - - - - - - - - - - - -

_____

Ham

_____

- - - - - - - - - - - - - - - - - -

_____

Ram

_____

- - - - - - - - - - - - - - - - - -

_____

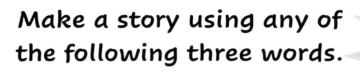

Make a story using any of the following three words. **'am'**

Jam   Yam   Cram   Tram

Ham   Ram   Clam   Dam

Pam   Sam   Slam

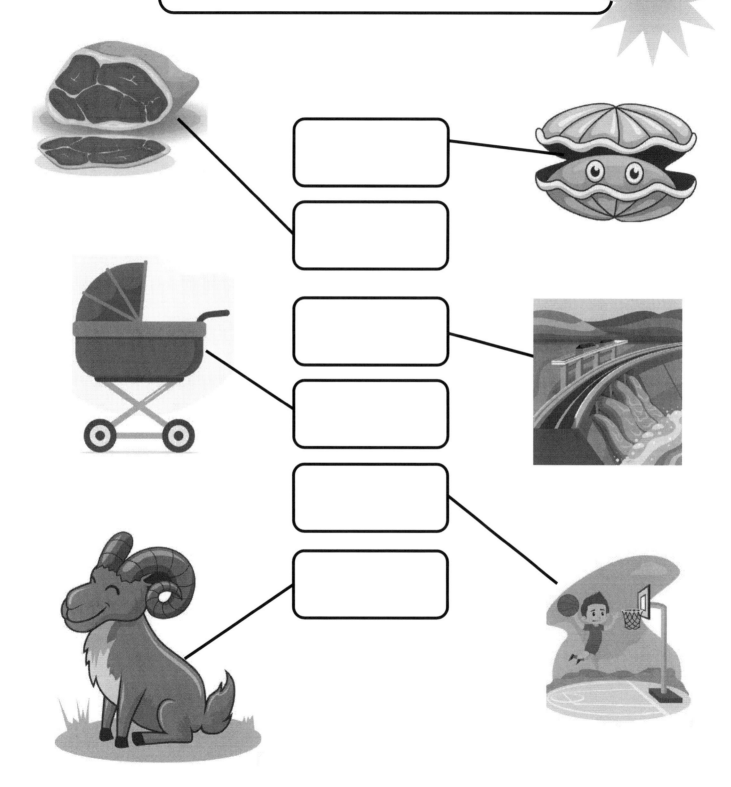

Write the name of each picture and listen to the ending sound. Circle 'amp' or 'am'.

'am'

am amp	am amp	am amp
am amp	am amp	am amp
am amp	am amp	am amp

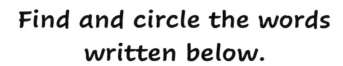

Find and circle the words written below.

'am'

clam	slam	ham	yam
tram	glam	dam	ram

h	r	c	l	t	c	k	g
s	d	a	m	p	a	k	l
p	a	m	w	r	a	m	a
t	c	p	l	l	v	a	m
m	a	m	p	l	n	s	a
a	l	a	m	h	l	i	r
l	s	t	r	a	m	p	t
c	s	l	a	m	a	y	t

The clan of misfits

Once upon a time, there was a small clan of misfits who had been exiled from their homelands. They were desperate to find some place they could call home, so they pooled together all their resources and made a plan. The man in charge assembled his loyal followers into an old, beat-up van, and they set out on the open road.

Along the way, they stopped to rest at a small inn where they met an old man with a big fan. He explained that he was part of a large clan and invited them to join his family. The desperate misfits were elated by this kind offer and quickly accepted it.

The man and his followers were welcomed by the entire clan with open arms and made to feel at home. They all worked together to build a new home for themselves using only what was available in the area. Everyone contributed, from the smallest child to the oldest member of the clan.

When it came time to finish off their new home, the clan came up with a plan. They gathered all the resources they had available and made one large pan. After long weeks of hard work and determination, their home was finished and looked better than ever!

The man in charge and his loyal followers were so relieved to finally have a place they could call home. The big fan had been a blessing for them, and they were all tan with happiness. They had run out of luck before, but this time was different. The clan was now united in one big happy family thanks to their plan and the old man's fan.

Write all the 'an' words that you have found in the story.				

The clan of misfits

- Once upon a time, there was a small _____ of misfits who had been exiled from their homelands.
- They pooled together all their resources and made a _____.
- The man in charge assembled his loyal followers into an old, beat-up _____.
- Along the way, they stopped to rest at a small inn where they met an old _____ with a big fan.
- He explained that he was part of a large _____ and invited them to join his family.
- Everyone contributed, from the smallest child to the oldest member of the _____.
- When it came time to finish off their new home, the clan came up with a _____.
- They gathered all the resources they had available and made one large _____.
- The big fan had been a blessing for them, and they were all _____ with happiness

Write any ten 'an' words.				

Read the story and circle whether the statement is true or false. If the statement is false, provide the correct answer for it.

There was a small village of misfits.

True   False

_____

They were desperate to find a hidden treasure.

True   False

_____

The man assembled his loyal followers into a car.

True   False

_____

They stopped to rest at a small inn where they met an old man with a big can.

True   False

_____
_____

They made one large pan.

True   False

_____

Read the story 'The clan of misfits' and answer the following questions.

'an'

What is the story about?

_____
_____
_____
_____

What was the clan in desperate need of?

_____
_____
_____
_____

Whom did they meet at the small inn?

_____
_____
_____
_____

How did they make their home and who helped them?

_____
_____
_____
_____

Once upon a time, there was a small clan of misfits who had been exiled from their homelands.	18
They were desperate to find some place they could call home, so they pooled together all their resources and made a plan.	22
The man in charge assembled his loyal followers into an old, beat-up van, and they set out on the open road.	61
Along the way, they stopped to rest at a small inn where they met an old man with a big fan.	82
He explained that he was part of a large clan and invited them to join his family.	99
The desperate misfits were elated by this kind offer and quickly accepted it.	112
The man and his followers were welcomed by the entire clan with open arms and made to feel at home.	132
They all worked together to build a new home for themselves using only what was available in the area.	151
Everyone contributed, from the smallest child to the oldest member of the clan.	164
When it came time to finish off their new home, the clan came up with a plan.	181
They gathered all the resources they had available and made one large pan.	195
After long weeks of hard work and determination, their home was finished and looked better than ever!	211
The man in charge and his loyal followers were so relieved to finally have a place they could call home.	231
The big fan had been a blessing for them, and they were all tan with happiness.	247
They had run out of luck before, but this time was different. The clan was now united in one big happy family thanks to their plan and the old man's fan.	279

Date			
Words per minute			
Number of Errors			

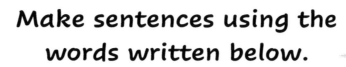

Make sentences using the
words written below.

'an'

Pan

_____
- -
_____

Man

_____
- -
_____

Tan

_____
- -
_____

Can

_____
- -
_____

Ran

_____
- -
_____

Ram

_____
- -
_____

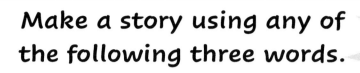

Make a story using any of the following three words. 'an'

Pan   Man   Can   Clan

Fan   Plan   Ran   Tan

Scan   Span   Began

_____

_____

_____

_____

_____

_____

_____

_____

_____

_____

_____

_____

_____

_____

_____

_____

'an'

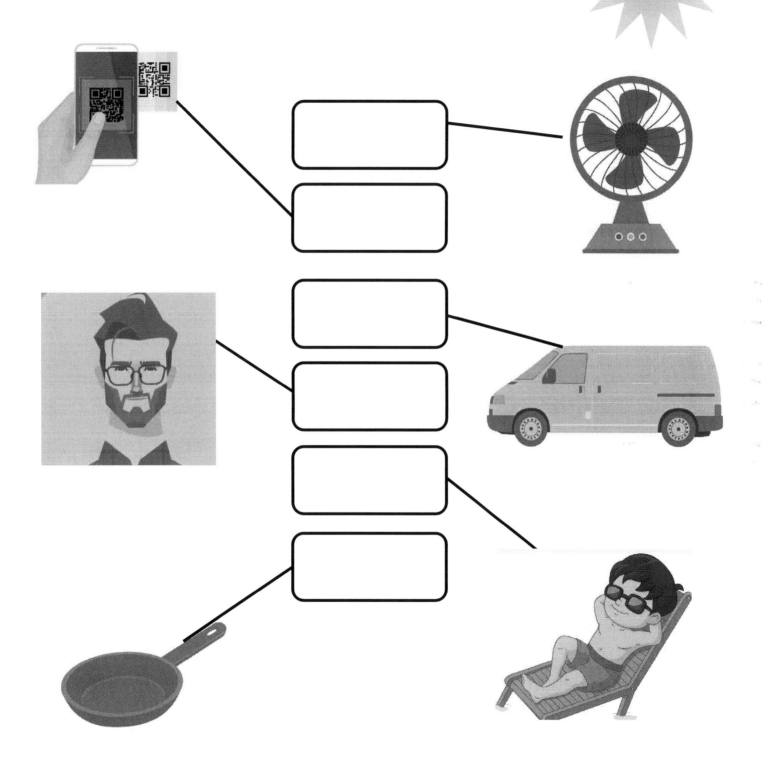

Write the name of each picture and listen to the ending sound. Circle 'an' or 'am'.

'an'

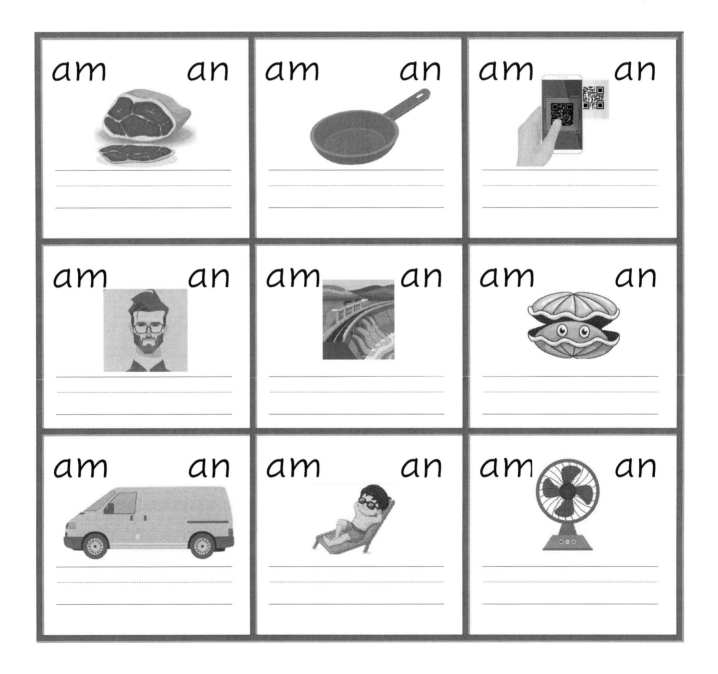

am an	am an	am an
_____	_____	_____
am an	am an	am an
_____	_____	_____
am an	am an	am an
_____	_____	_____

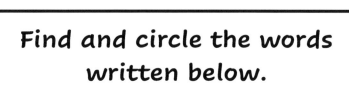

Find and circle the words written below.

'an'

man   ran   van   tan   can

lan   plan   scan   fan

p	l	a	n	t	f	k	g
s	c	a	n	p	a	k	v
p	l	a	n	r	n	m	a
t	c	p	l	l	v	a	n
m	a	m	p	l	n	s	a
n	t	a	n	h	l	r	r
a	s	t	r	a	m	a	t
c	s	l	a	m	a	n	t

Read the story. Identify and underline all the 'ap' words.   'ap'

Alex's nap

Alex was strolling along the beach with his map in hand, looking for the perfect spot to take a nap. As he walked, he heard a faint tapping coming from one of the coves ahead. He cautiously made his way closer and saw an old woman sitting on a rock and tapping her foot against the ground.

He was about to turn and leave when she suddenly snapped her fingers and waved him over. He hesitated for a moment, but then went closer with curiosity. She greeted him in an oddly familiar voice and asked him why he was there.

Alex explained that he had been looking for a place to take a nap and showed the woman his map. She smiled and told him there was a perfect spot not too far from where they were standing. She pointed to a gap between two rocks, just big enough for a person to get through.

Alex thanked the old woman and made his way toward the gap she had shown him. He glanced around, making sure he wasn't being watched, and quickly made his way through the gap and into a small clearing. He saw a narrow beach, surrounded by tall trees on one side and huge rocks on the other.

The sun was setting, casting a beautiful golden light over everything. Alex grinned as he spread out his blanket and prepared to take a nap. As he lay down, he felt himself being lulled to sleep by the gentle sound of waves lapping against the shore.

When he woke up, Alex felt more relaxed than ever before. He stretched and smiled, feeling the warm sun on his skin. He quickly rolled up his blanket and made his way back through the gap, feeling grateful for the old woman's directions. As he walked back towards the main beach, he felt a sense of accomplishment, having found the perfect spot for his nap. He couldn't wait to come back and do it all again!

Write all the 'ap' words that you have found in the story.				

Read the story and fill in the blank spaces with the appropriate words.

'ap'

Alex's nap

- Alex was strolling along the beach with his _____ in hand.
- Looking for the perfect spot to take a _____.
- As he walked, he heard a faint _____ping coming from one of the coves ahead.
- He cautiously made his way closer and saw an old woman sitting on a rock and _____ping her foot against the ground.
- He was about to turn and leave when she suddenly _____ped her fingers and waved him over.
- Alex explained that he had been looking for a place to take a _____ and showed the woman his map.
- She pointed to a _____ between two rocks, just big enough for a person to get through.
- Alex thanked the old woman and made his way toward the _____ she had shown him.
- As he lay down, he felt himself being lulled to sleep by the gentle sound of waves _____ping against the shore.

Write any ten 'ap' words.				

82

Read the story and circle whether the statement is true or false. If the statement is false, provide the correct answer for it.

'ap'

Alex was looking for a place to take a nap on the beach.

True   False

_____

The old woman pointed him towards a gap between two rocks.

True   False

_____

The environment in the small clearing was bustling and noisy.

True   False

_____

Alex felt uneasy when the old woman snapped her fingers.

True   False

_____

Alex was disappointed when he woke up from his nap.

True   False

_____

Alex felt himself being lulled to sleep by the gentle sound of song.

True   False

_____

What was Alex looking for when he was strolling along the beach?

What did the old woman show him when he told her his purpose?

What was the environment like in the small clearing that Alex found through the gap between two rocks?

Was the old woman surprised when Alex showed her his map?

Assess the fluency by writing the number of words read per minute.

'ap'

Alex was strolling along the beach with his map in hand, looking for the perfect spot to take a nap.	20
As he walked, he heard a faint tapping coming from one of the coves ahead.	35
He cautiously made his way closer and saw an old woman sitting on a rock and tapping her foot against the ground.	57
He was about to turn and leave when she suddenly snapped her fingers and waved him over.	74
He hesitated for a moment, but then went closer with curiosity.	85
She greeted him in an oddly familiar voice and asked him why he was there.	100
Alex explained that he had been looking for a place to take a nap and showed the woman his map.	120
She smiled and told him there was a perfect spot not too far from where they were standing.	138
She pointed to a gap between two rocks, just big enough for a person to get through.	155
Alex thanked the old woman and made his way toward the gap she had shown him.	171
He glanced around, making sure he wasn't being watched, and quickly made his way through the gap and into a small clearing.	196
He saw a narrow beach, surrounded by tall trees on one side and huge rocks on the other.	214
The sun was setting, casting a beautiful golden light over everything.	234
Alex grinned as he spread out his blanket and prepared to take a nap.	250
As he lay down, he felt himself being lulled to sleep by the gentle sound of waves lapping against the shore.	260
When he woke up, Alex felt more relaxed than ever before.	271
He stretched and smiled, feeling the warm sun on his skin.	282
He quickly rolled up his blanket and made his way back through the gap, feeling grateful for the old woman's directions.	303
As he walked back towards the main beach, he felt a sense of accomplishment, having found the perfect spot for his nap. He couldn't wait to come back and do it all again!	336

Date			
Words per minute			
Number of Errors			

Cap

_____
- -
_____

Tap

_____
- -
_____

Lap

_____
- -
_____

Rap

_____
- -
_____

Nap

_____
- -
_____

Clap

_____
- -
_____

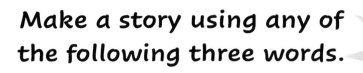

Make a story using any of the following three words. 'ap'

Clap Snap Crap Tap Lap

Rap Nap Tap Map Cap

Gap Tap Flap

_____

_____

_____

_____

_____

_____

_____

_____

_____

_____

_____

_____

'ap'

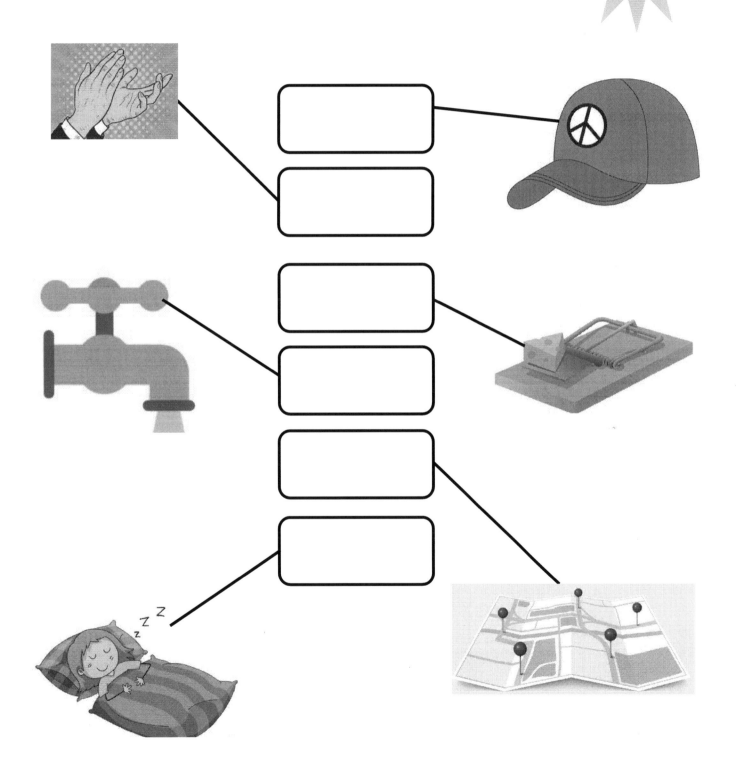

Write the name of each picture and listen to the ending sound. Circle 'an' or 'ap'.

'ap'

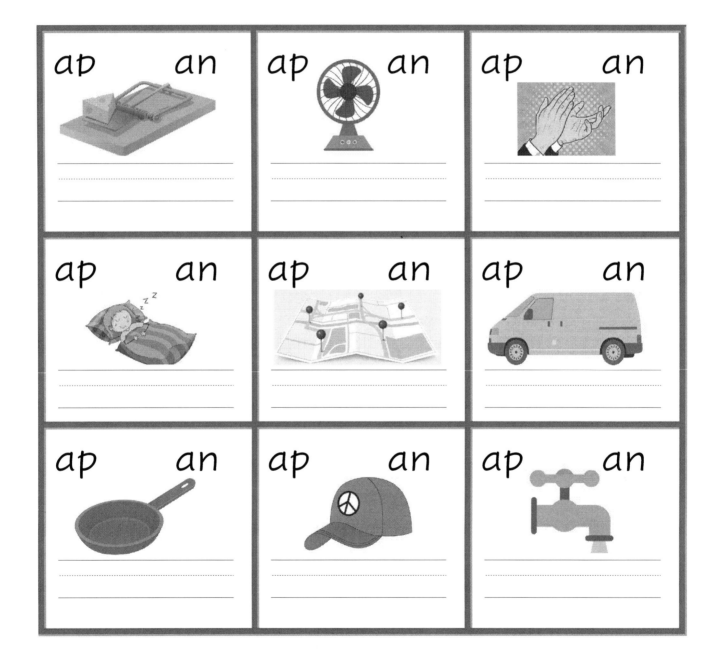

ap an	ap an	ap an
ap an	ap an	ap an
ap an	ap an	ap an

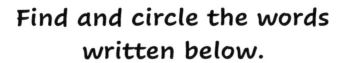

Find and circle the words written below.

'ap'

clap   tap   lap   nap   trap
flap   map   cap   wrap

p	l	c	w	r	a	p	f
s	a	a	n	p	a	k	l
p	l	m	n	r	n	m	a
t	c	p	l	l	v	a	p
m	a	m	p	l	n	s	a
n	t	a	t	h	l	r	r
a	s	t	a	a	m	a	t
c	l	a	p	a	n	n	t

Read the story. Identify and underline all the 'nd' words.

'nd'

The power of the wind

John was walking through a beautiful field of land, taking in the sight and sound of nature around him. He couldn't help but feel fond of this place as he walked through the soft sand beneath his feet. Suddenly, something caught his eye. A glimmering object just beyond the edge of a pond seemed to be calling out to him. He ventured closer to take a look, and as he reached out his hand, he felt an overwhelming urge to find it.

He walked around the pond, feeling the grass crunching beneath his feet as he looked for the object. With each step, John became more determined to find whatever had caught his eye. Soon enough, he stumbled upon it, buried beneath a pile of sand. He quickly picked it up and brushed the dirt off to get a better look. To his surprise, it was an old grindstone!

John marveled at his discovery and ran his hand along its surface. He felt something strange on the side of the grindstone and carefully wiped away more sand to reveal a small plaque. It read "Bind what cannot be seen and find what is hidden in the wind". John was filled with curiosity as he tried to figure out this mysterious message.

He carefully trudged back to his house, grindstone in hand, and began to research its origin. After days of looking, he finally came across an old book with a similar message inscribed on the cover. It said, "The power of the wind is strong and blind. Bind what cannot be seen and find what is hidden."

John realized that the grindstone held great importance, but he still didn't understand how to use it. After days spent in contemplation, John was finally able to unlock the power of the grindstone. He had discovered the secret to the wind's invisible force, and he couldn't help but feel proud.

With his newfound knowledge, John has been using it to bind what cannot be seen and find what is hidden in the wind. He now understands that sometimes, even things that appear as ordinary as a grindstone can hold extraordinary powers.

Write all the 'nd' words that you have found in the story.				

Read the story and fill in the blank spaces with the appropriate words.

'nd'

The power of the wind

- John was walking through a beautiful field of _____, taking in the sight and _____ of nature _____ him.
- He couldn't help but feel _____ of this place as he walked through the soft _____ beneath his feet.
- He ventured closer to take a look, and as he reached out his _____, he felt an overwhelming urge to _____ it.
- He walked around the _____, feeling the grass crunching beneath his feet as he looked for the object.
- Soon enough, he stumbled upon it, buried beneath a pile of _____.
- John marveled at his discovery and ran his _____ along its surface.
- _____ what cannot be seen and _____ what is hidden in the _____.
- He carefully trudged back to his house, grindstone in _____, and began to research its origin.
- The power of the _____ is strong and _____. _____ what cannot be seen and _____ what is hidden.
- John has been using it to _____ what cannot be seen and _____ what is hidden in the _____.

Write any ten 'nd' words.				

Read the story and circle whether the statement is true or false. If the statement is false, provide the correct answer for it.

'nd'

John found a grindstone at the edge of the pond.

True   False

_____

_____

The power of the wind is weak and blind.

True   False

_____

_____

The grindstone contained an ordinary message.

True   False

_____

_____

John was able to unlock the power of the grindstone immediately after finding it.

True   False

_____

_____

_____

_____

John is using his newfound knowledge to find what cannot be seen.

True   False

_____

_____

Read the story 'The power of the wind' and answer the following questions.

'nd'

What did John find at the edge of the pond?

What message was inscribed on the grindstone's plaque?

How did John unlock the power of the grindstone?

What is John now using his newfound knowledge for?

Assess the fluency by writing the number of words read per minute.

'nd'

John was walking through a beautiful field of land, taking in the sight and sound of nature around him.	19
He couldn't help but feel fond of this place as he walked through the soft sand beneath his feet.	38
Suddenly, something caught his eye.	43
A glimmering object just beyond the edge of a pond seemed to be calling out to him.	60
He ventured closer to take a look, and as he reached out his hand, he felt an overwhelming urge to find it.	82
He walked around the pond, feeling the grass crunching beneath his feet as he looked for the object.	100
With each step, John became more determined to find whatever had caught his eye.	115
Soon enough, he stumbled upon it, buried beneath a pile of sand.	126
He quickly picked it up and brushed the dirt off to get a better look.	141
To his surprise, it was an old grindstone! John marveled at his discovery and ran his hand along its surface.	162
He felt something strange on the side of the grindstone and carefully wiped away more sand to reveal a small plaque.	182
It read "Bind what cannot be seen and find what is hidden in the wind".	197
John was filled with curiosity as he tried to figure out this mysterious message.	211
He carefully trudged back to his house, grindstone in hand, and began to research its origin.	227
After days of looking, he finally came across an old book with a similar message inscribed on the cover.	246
It said, "The power of the wind is strong and blind. Bind what cannot be seen and find what is hidden."	267
John realized that the grindstone held great importance, but he still didn't understand how to use it.	284
After days spent in contemplation, John was finally able to unlock the power of the grindstone.	300
He had discovered the secret to the wind's invisible force, and he couldn't help but feel proud.	317
With his newfound knowledge, John has been using it to bind what cannot be seen and find what is hidden in the wind.	340
He now understands that sometimes, even things that appear as ordinary as a grindstone can hold extraordinary powers.	358

Date			
Words per minute			
Number of Errors			

Make sentences using the words written below.

'nd'

Pond

_____

- -

_____

Wind

_____

- -

_____

Find

_____

- -

_____

Sand

_____

- -

_____

Hand

_____

- -

_____

Land

_____

- -

_____

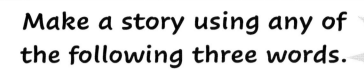

Make a story using any of the following three words. 'nd'

Pond   Wind   Find   Sand

Hand   Land   Around

Pond   Bind   Kind

_____

_____

_____

_____

_____

_____

_____

_____

_____

_____

_____

_____

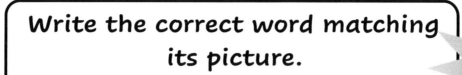

Write the correct word matching its picture.

'nd'

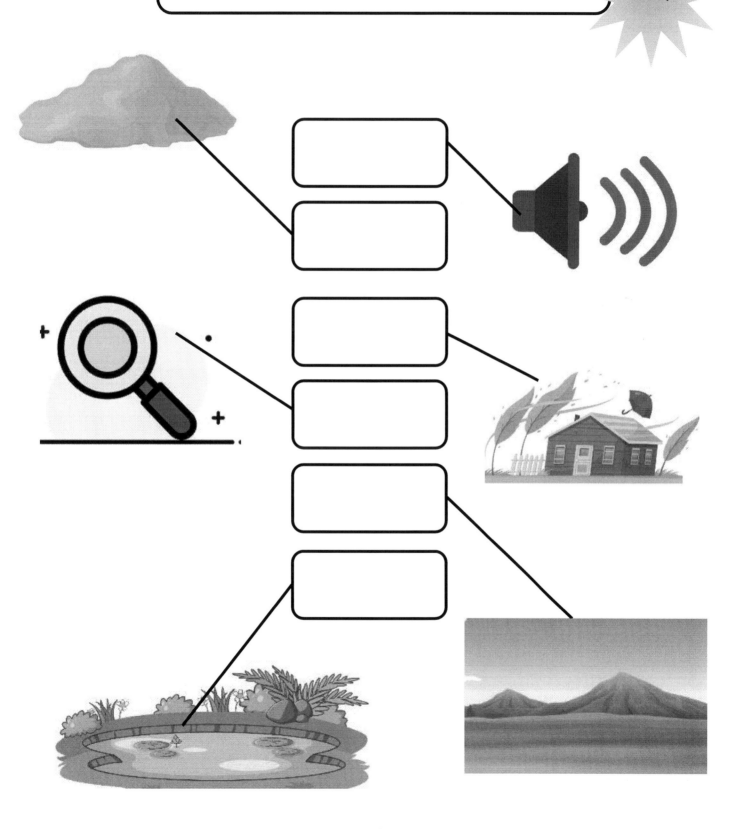

Write the name of each picture and listen to the ending sound. Circle 'an' or 'nd'.

'nd'

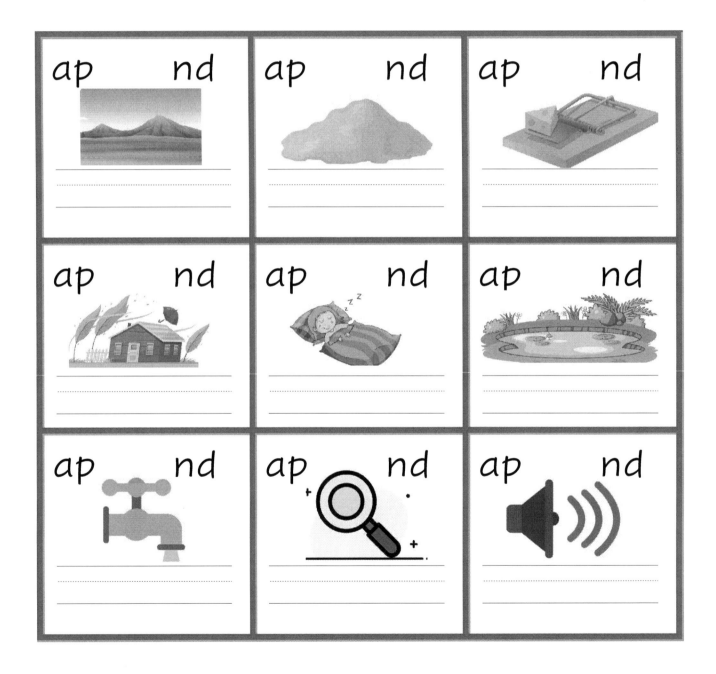

ap	nd	ap	nd	ap	nd

ap	nd	ap	nd	ap	nd

ap	nd	ap	nd	ap	nd

Find and circle the words written below.

'nd'

wind   bind   grind   sound
around   land   found

p	l	c	w	r	a	p	f
s	o	u	n	d	a	k	l
p	m	l	a	n	d	m	a
f	o	u	n	d	v	a	d
m	a	m	p	l	n	s	n
n	t	a	t	h	l	r	i
a	s	t	a	a	m	a	r
w	i	n	d	n	i	b	g

Made in the USA
Monee, IL
30 April 2023

32724858R00059